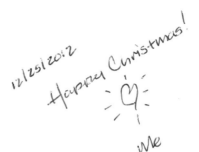

HOPE
IN THE FORM
OF STRIPES

minerva
Editor

Karen Lewis
Associate Editor

Marie Altman and Cathy Barber
Field Editors

2006
California Poets in the Schools
Statewide Anthology

Cover art by Blake More

Book design by Laurence Brauer

Typography by Wordsworth, San Geronimo, CA

Printing by McNaughton & Gunn, Saline, MI

ISBN 0-939927-22-5

To order copies of *Hope in the Form of Stripes*, contact:
California Poets in the Schools
Phone: 415-221-4201
Email: info@cpits.org
www.cpits.org

*This anthology is dedicated to the
many volunteers, poet-teachers, and board members
who believe in the future of California Poets in the Schools.*

Special Thanks to Terri Glass.

California Poets in the Schools is grateful to the hundreds of individuals, foundations and agencies who graciously offer their support:

Margo Eachus
Corinne Eding
Jane Elsdon
Mark & Laura Epstein-Norris
Sandra Erickson
Roy & Elizabeth Haas Eisenhardt
Lawrence Ferlinghetti
LaKeesha Gage
J. Ruth Gendler
Marilyn Gevirtz
Paula Gocker
George Goddard
Dale & Phillip Going
Dina Vest Goodman
Louis & Sandra Handler
Susan Hartz
Lyn Hejinian
Barbara Holmes
Paul & Maxine Hoover
Torre Houlgate-West
Carol Ireland & Uncle Don Ireland
Robin Jacobson
Valerie Johns
George & Sylvia Johnson
Debra Johnson
Barbara Jourdonnais
William & Patricia Klussman
Jennifer Miller Kristel
Gerrett Snedaker & Diane Krause
Hut Landon
Richard Delwiche & Dawn Larkin
Gyönge Laky & Thomas Layton
Nancy Leavens
Jesse & Joanne Levy
Barbara Lewis
Nina Lindsay
Colleen Lookingbill
Lynn & David Loux
Leon & Helen Sloss Luey
Jim & Megan Mackintosh
Lynda Malavanya
Allen Tinker & Arlene Mayerson
Nion McEvoy
Ira Polcyn McEvoy
Eliska Meyers

Janice Mirikitani
Diane Moore
Trudy Baltz & Christopher Motley
Nancy Newmeyer
Gwynn O'Gara
Mike & Judy O'Shea
Diane & Donald Onken
Ruth Palmer
Ruth Palnee
Rabbi Stephen Pearce
Neal Powers
Lynne Rappaport
Barbara & Nigel Renton
Mary Lou Robinson
John Robinson
Ivy & Leigh Robinson
Cynthia Anne & John Roe
Susan & Raymond Roegiers
Robert & Sharon Ross
Robert & Joan Saffa
Denis & Kristine Salmon
Dr. Bruce Sams
Susie Schlesinger
Ruth Scott
C. David Scronce
Karol Sinicki & Julian Sinai
Kevin & Lynn Slobodien
Jessie & Barbara Smith
Joan Marler Smith
Neal Sofman
Anne Stenzel
Robert & Laura Stewart
Gretchen Stone
Gregory Sykes
Edith & Robert Tannenbaum
Lyn Taylor
David & Susan Terris
Valerie Walker
Malcolm & Karen Whyte
George & Sara Williams
Jim & Elaine Wolf
Susan Wooldridge
Janet Young
Dr. Glen Young
Patti Zussman

SPECIAL THANKS TO THE FOUNDATIONS AND ORGANIZATIONS WHO MADE THIS
ANTHOLOGY POSSIBLE

Barbara Smith & The Borun Foundation
Marin Poets in the Schools
National Endowment for the Arts

NATIONAL
ENDOWMENT
FOR THE ARTS

WE WISH TO ACKNOWLEDGE THE SUPPORT OF THE FOLLOWING GOVERNMENT,
CORPORATE AND FOUNDATION SUPPORTERS WHO HAVE MADE OUR POETRY
RESIDENCIES, ANTHOLOGIES AND CONFERENCES POSSIBLE.

Bay Area Rapid Transit & East Bay Community Foundation
    Tiny Tickets Program
Books, Inc.
California Arts Council
City Lights Foundation
The Community Thrift Store
The Congregation Emanu-El
Entrekin Family Foundation
e-Scrip
W. A. Gerbode Foundation
The Grove Consultants International
The Walter & Elise Haas Fund
Marin Arts Council
Marin Community Foundation
Mervyn's
Miranda Lux Foundation
National Endowment for the Arts
New Vision Foundation
Orrick, Herrington & Sutcliffe
Potrero Nuevo Fund
Silver Giving Foundation
The Starbucks Foundation
St. Paul's Companies, Inc. Foundation
The Walton Family Foundation
Wendell Family Fund
Zellerbach Family Fund
Zyzzyva

California

Arts Council

Contents

KEEPING OUR WORDS ALIVE
STUDENT POEMS

WE CELEBRATE OUR POET SELVES
POET-TEACHER POEMS

ESSAYS AND LESSON PLANS

Introduction

What do you think of when you think of stripes — these thin places in between?

Do you think of long straight lines? Or, flat, narrow or thin bands of contrasting color well placed in between its surroundings? It could be a sweep of the paintbrush or a long straight mark of a pencil upon a clean white page.

No doubt about it, stripes stand out. Or, stripes may whisper. Looking to the left, looking to the right, there is not another around. To be a stripe you have to be an individual.

There is much hope in the form of a stripe.

To be a stripe you have to live, like a poem, inside your possibilities. And a poem is a lot like hope.

Hope and poems are all around. Poets know that. They go into small thin places where poetry lives. They tunnel below the surface of things to mine meaning and make discoveries. "Eureka! A Poem At Last!!"

California Poets in the Schools (CPITS) knows this, too. That is why this program exists. For more than 40 years, CPITS has strategically placed poets in classrooms to teach and to work with students to help them recognize and celebrate the poetry that lives inside each of us.

This collection of poems by these gifted young poets and their poet-teachers is CPITS' celebration of creativity, intuition, and curiosity. Encouraging students to write using their life experience and their own special perceptions to create poetry is like sending forth many rays of light out into the world. You will see what power has been created in the pages that follow. These poems are so honest and full of hope. These poems are lovely, beautiful, and delightful. Savor them.

Reading "Hope" by John Gregario, I see what power and hope there are in stripes. "Hope is a wise monk / meditating on a clear silent hill / bald and peaceful, seeking / answers, asking himself / many questions, wanting / an answer to stopping wars."

When I read Michael Villanueva's poem "Ode to Bach," bold, broad-banded stripes filled my thoughts. "As jagged as a knife, the violin stroke / Upbeat, excited, thunderous / Yet smooth as a cool ocean breeze / Calming the soul."

When I was asked to write the introduction to this collection, I felt so proud and honored, and just a little bit nervous. After all, I am a writer of stories, not a poet. As I read all the poems, I was struck by the powerful stories within them. Pay attention to what you read, what you see. Thin narrow bands can trick the eye. Deliberately placed, stripes mystify the viewer.

Stripes hide things. Camouflage. And the viewer may not even get the chance to see what they thought they were looking at because the thing they thought they saw is gone — in a flash, like a clownfish, like a zebra. Or, a tiger as you will see in Rowan Cunningham's poem "The Tiger of the Little Spirit." "The tiger of the little spirit / lay in the summer air."

When I think of poems and stripes, I think of patterns. I think of lines and forms that repeat and repeat. I think of ribbons of color and splashes of flashing light across a steel gray sky. If I were a stripe, I would be a rainbow stripe; only all the colors would do for me. Rita Volkovinskaya describes this in her poem "Ode to Lapis Lazuli." She shows us there is hope in the form of stripes. "Your thick blue stripes scattered across your body / like the morbid night . . . And when I hold you / I hold all of the almighty heavens."

Good poems go on forever. Good poems, like the poems in this collection, will make you want to read them again and again. You can climb into the small thin places in between where poetry lives and breathes. It takes just one breath. This is where hope lives.

Imagine the pattern your feet make in the path where you walk as I did when I read Luke Morrison's poem, "Poetry." ". . . Poetry is / the footprints that follow me / on my journey home."

Like a stripe, poetry does not often blend in with the environment. And, when it does, a poem could leap out and pounce meaning all around you. The poems in this anthology are full of possibilities and meaning. Poems and stripes and hopes are so very necessary indeed.

Jerdine Nolen
Children's author
Ellicott City, Maryland
May 2005

Hope in the Form of Stripes

"We never want to be in the position of having to kill an animal."
— Mike Wintemute, Fish and Game spokesman, 2/26/05

Less than a mile from my house,
in one of the rare, wild, open spaces
that called my family to the Conejo Valley
from the tumultuous traffic
and sprawl of Hollywood,
came a cat, creeping and casting life
into my bored suburban imagination.

His rumor spread quickly, jumping freeways like the Fire of 2003.
On Tuesday a rancher reported
a glimpse of feline — too large for lynx or bobcat —
darting into the brush near the Reagan Library.
He was the talk of our rabbit-ridden valley for days:
Was he a hoax, a ghost of hope, maybe even Ronnie
returned to earth as the MGM Lion resurrected?

By Friday wildlife officials found fresh tracks
in rain-soaked Thousand Oaks earth,
six inches wide and seven inches long.
"A captive African Lion escaped, they said,
maybe as large as 600 pounds."
So they set baits with fresh goat meat
while desperate housewives kept babies and bunnies inside.

Saturday I sipped coffee and stared through my window
a flimsy wall of glass barricading me from
acres of hills thigh-high in rye where tall tails could hide.
I longed for large copper eyes to stare me down,
a padded paw to swipe at the squalling scrub jay,
a golden mane to peer in splendor, then pounce through the grass
and jolt me to a holy place where we could roam together as one.

By Sunday he'd tell me of his majestic sufferings,
His delight at unfenced plains, his fear of cages,
His distrust of animals who believed
in their dominion over every living thing.
I searched for words to settle his doubts
and promised to keep him from any harm
But we both knew how eloquently words could lie.

In days and nights to come I dreamed of cats,
even rode a white tiger through the surf.
He spoke to me of peace, and the wisdom
of ancient saber-tooths who roared mightily
yet never abandoned their injured brothers.
Calling me "sister" he told me to cover my heart with glass
So I could see truth and not be scarred by it.

Black and orange stripes were spotted on Thursday,
in a ravine behind a house not far from the Target store.
Helicopters wrangled the beast, who cowered from the noise,
Shots rang through the open space; shook and spilled cups of coffee
from a neighbor's porch.
Robe-clad on-lookers watched hunters net and dead lift
a rare Siberian Tiger into a waiting flatbed truck.

I chopped down the tall ryegrass on my hillside that day,
knowing the cat would no longer need it to hide in.
With every chop I swung at the officials who killed instead of tranquilized,
swung at the owner, who has yet to come forward and claim him,
swung when the necropsy pronounced him young, healthy, and declawed
with nothing but hairballs in his stomach,
swung at a society that increasingly shoots — then thinks.

I raged at the loss of hope in the form of stripes,
the loss of bright-burning imagination
and chopped, chopped,
chopped,
until I heard glass crack
and a woman's heart
roar.

Lucia Lemieux
Ventura County

Keeping Our Words Alive

Student Poems

The Tiger of the Little Spirit

The tiger of the little spirit
lay in the summer air.
He is shedding his fur.
He gazes at the glittering, full moon.
It is shining as brightly as the sun.
Then he gets up.
His glittering coat
shines in the dark.

Rowan Cunningham
Grade 2, Liberty Elementary School, Sonoma County
Katie Lundy, Classroom Teacher
Molly Albracht, Poet-Teacher

Love

Love is a hopeful whisper
in your house at night.
You think it's a voice
but it's love.

Tyler Ross
Grade 3, Liberty Elementary School, Sonoma County
Laura Berg, Classroom Teacher
Molly Albracht, Poet-Teacher

My New Street

On my street
Leaves are falling and
Turning into puddles.
The people on my
Street are always
Feeling down so when I
Ask them to play ball
They quietly say no
And shut the door
Slowly. I always
Eat a plum, apple or lemon or
Ice cream. The
People on my street
Only eat bread, cold
Bread. If a big fire
Would happen they
Would slowly walk
Down the street to the fire
Station. That's my street.

Jennifer Lynne Shearer
Grade 3, Highlands Elementary School, San Mateo County
After School Enrichment Program
Cathy Barber, Poet-Teacher

Poetry

Poetry is an owl inside a secret
rock of fog. Poetry is life
rapping when thunder howls.
Poetry is the roots of stone
where I emerge. Poetry is
the footprints that follow me
on my journey home.
Poetry is the stars I see at night;
the peace and terror I cannot run from.
Poetry is the song in my heart,
the dance in my soul.

Luke Morrison
Grade 5, Neil Cummins School, Marin County
Frank Shippey, Classroom Teacher
Karen Benke, Poet-Teacher

A Tornado of Friendship

A cloud bursting into scraps of wind,
A big hole with blue air swirling inside it.
Thin cotton streaming through my fingers,
Milk filling my throat.
A gift of kindness blowing in the open sky.
A bird of loneliness surveying its nest.
A smile spreading on one's face.
A tornado of friendship.

Sophie Smith
Grade 3, Neil Cummins School, Marin County
Meredith Abramowitz, Classroom Teacher
Sasha Eakle, Poet-Teacher

Three Poems

it was
just a drizzle
now it's rain.

Raining on
a pole
with Chinese letters.

Smells
like mint
falling down.

Elizabeth Anguiano
Grade 3, Neil Cummins School, Marin County
Colleen Beery, Classroom Teacher
Sasha Eakle, Poet-Teacher

Autumn

Autumn covers me in acorns.
The nut-brown squirrels surround me
as they race for a hollow tree
just as the midnight black forest starts to blaze.
The dandelion clouds drop sky blue rain.
Oh God, open me,
look in my heart.
Blanket me in love,
drown in joy
The leaves of sunlight and fire fall,
the rusty orange and brown leaves drop.
Give me the fluffy fog
Bring me the white frost.

Sam Steinhauer
Grade 4, Lynwood School, Marin County
Lori Marston, Classroom Teacher
Terri Glass, Poet-Teacher

A Grain of Sand

Being a grain of sand is way harder
than anything you've done.
So small against the world,
so helpless against the wind.
Being swept up and blown away
to a place you've never been.
Getting stuck to somebody's wet foot
or bathing suit.
What's worse, you humans get to die,
but sand lives forever.
There's no end to our misery.
There's no heaven to look forward to.
No end.
No nothing.
Everybody thinks one tiny grain of sand
makes a difference.
Well, it doesn't.
It doesn't make you get an "A,"
or improve your luck.
It does nothing.
We do nothing.
And we'll keep on doing nothing
and being nothing
long, long after you die.
We don't have families.
Don't have anybody to look after us.
We're all alone in the world.
No one.
Nobody.

Elizabeth Avina
Grade 5, Rivergold School, Madera County
Mary Lee Gowland, Poet-Teacher

Rainfalls

When the rain falls I hear my
ancestors speaking

When the wind blows I can
see my ancestor spinning

When the sun shines I can
see my ancestor's mouth form a grin

When the water flows I can
hear my ancestor singing

When the flower blooms I can
hear my ancestors thinking

When the leaves turn red I can
see their spirits rise to the heavens

When the lightning flashes
I know they are angry

When cliffs turn into mountains
I see them growing

When the beetles walk along the earth
I know they are walking

When the shells and rocks form a circle
on the beach I know
they're sharing messages

When the rain falls I can
hear them speaking

Charlotte Benz
Grade 3, Lakeshore Alternative Elementary School
Oliver Glover, Classroom Teacher
Grace Grafton, Poet-Teacher

Jealousy

I am the feeling you get when you think
Someone is better than you

You feel like the bunny that can't hop
When I visit you

I show up when a girl thinks she's
Not as beautiful as another

You feel like one of the broken toys
When I touch you

When you feel lonely and left out
I'm there

When everybody else can go on a trip
You feel me

I visit when you're the
Last one in line

You're touched by me when you
Want another's clothes

I'm there when someone else
Has what you wanted

I am something you don't want
I am Jealousy

Eileen Sandoval
Grade 4, Weathersfield Elementary
Sheri Leiken, Classroom Teacher
Lucia Lemieux, Poet-Teacher

Ode to the Arts

Dedicated to the people who help bring arts to kids like me

Oh, Arts, you are the light that dances through the rain
You are like the oxygen I breathe.
Oh, Arts, your many expressive ways
enlighten everyone.
I remember when you first shook my hand,
and your creativity flowed into my heart!
Oh, Arts, I thank you for letting me daydream
about singing on a stage,
or swimming in a pool of words.
To me, you are the morning light,
waking everyone up.

Zoe Celeste Lemieux
Grade 5, Weathersfield Elementary
Beth Davis, Classroom Teacher
Lucia Lemieux, Poet-Teacher

The Indian Base

Hear the talk of my friends
Smell the smoked salmon from our hunt
Listen to the dribble of the rain

See the prints on my track
Hear the roar of my storm
Look into my dangerous face
You will never come near

My tepee cracks of fire
My birds sing of danger
I have been destroyed before
But I will not let it happen again.

Griffin Lucht
Grade 4, Weathersfield Elementary
Sheri Leikin, Classroom Teacher
Lucia Lemieux, Poet-Teacher

I Never Write About Anything

I never write
about anything like the color
of the darkness of midnight
Or how the veins in my body are like mazes
I never write
about anything because I don't like to write
Or maybe I'm afraid to write
about my true feelings
about life itself
I never write about anything.

Kyle Callen
Grade 7, Mendocino Middle School, Mendocino County
Dale Leister, Classroom Teacher
Karen Lewis, Poet-Teacher

A Whisper

Swish swish
crackle crackle boom boom
a thunder storm
beating dripping
lightning
thunder
the ocean left
this simple whisper
in a shell
I now listen
listen
quiet.

Anna Leach
Grade 4, Dan Gray Elementary, Mendocino County
Sally Miller, Classroom Teacher
Karen Lewis, Poet-Teacher

Rain

We thank you for water,
for your sound like fingers snapping
going click click.
Rain, you are so cool to fall
like water kicking my school.
You help us wash our hands,
to eat dinner, make jello,
lakes, showers to be clean
for school tomorrow.
Rain, do you ever need glasses
to see where you're going?
Why do you cry and make us wet?
Do you shout on top of roofs
I want to go back?
When people shake trees
and you fall off do you want to cry?
Rain, how come you never rise
to the sky? Rain do you ever get wet?
Rain, do you ever get lost
in this empty world? Do you
have some friends in the sky?
Do you make the sea grow?

Jesus Muñoz
Grade 3, Isla Vista School, Santa Barbara County
Ms. Montgomery, Classroom Teacher
Perie Longo, Poet-Teacher

Recipe for a Broken Heart

One gallon of heavy duty chunky
peanut butter

Three flowers to bloom in front of
your eyes

Mix four swans majestic and wise
5 cups of sunlight to burst

Stir in the mountain snowy
or not

Add one night of catching fireflies
under the willow and you have
mended a broken heart

Aubrey Macker
Grade 5, Cold Spring School, Santa Barbara County
Ms. Fargas, Classroom Teacher
Perie Longo, Poet-Teacher

How To Bring Winter

Go into a cold, snowy place and take a mouthful
of the freezing wind. Catch the first dew on a rose's
dark red petal and store it in a burning flame.
Keep it in the flame till night comes and steals
the light from day. Climb to the top of a mountain
and snatch the smallest rock. Wait on the top
of a hill until the darkest sunset comes and mix
the wind, the dew, and the rock in a soft fluffy
cloud. Go outside to your favorite place. Take
all the happiness and joy you've experienced there.
Then go to the highest place on earth and reach out
to the sky. Place the cloud that holds all the secret
ingredients in the palm of God's soothing hand
and winter shall come.

Alex Greer
Grade 5, Cold Spring School, Santa Barbara County
Mrs. Orwig, Classroom Teacher
Perie Longo, Poet-Teacher

Plain Prison

In my enclosure, a plain white room,
there are no details, no expressions, just white

There are two windows
where people gaze at me and wonder —
seeing such a plain girl in such a plain room.

A sudden burst of colors
breaks through one window and out the other.
Vivid hues I've seen before but never felt —

Pink like the roses next door, now I smell them,
Orange like the children's ball, now I embrace it.
Yellow like the canary in its cage downstairs, now I hear it.

Green like the front lawn, now I see it.
Blue like mom's blueberry muffins, now I taste them.
Violet like the color of my soul, so bright, yet so dark, now I show it.

I run toward the rainbow and slide down its colors,
out the window, out of my plain white prison.

Kat Brown
Grade 9, Ramona High, San Diego County
Connie Mendoza, Classroom Teacher
Seretta Martin, Poet-Teacher

Hello, Kids of Earth

How are you?
How, how is your ocean?
How is your family?
How is your mom, dad, brother or sister?
How are you holding out?
Are you hurt from the tornadoes,
or the earthquake?
How are you?

Devin Booth
Grade 4, Oak Grove School, Sonoma County
Terry Carroll, Classroom Teacher
Phyllis H. Meshulam, Poet-Teacher

My roots

In Taiwan
A coconut,
Freed from
Its palm tree,
Its mainland.
Thinking of others, thinking of you, thinking of family honor,
Doing what my ancestors want me to do for our everlasting cause,
Continue our ancient legacy, find our true meaning in the world.

Believe in	Hope	Fortune
Optimism	Health	Happiness
Every	family	brings
Pride	Honor	Love
Roads	Paths	Legacy
My	single	destiny
Is to	simply	succeed

And make it so that my ancestors give me
This chance, this determination, this
Honor, this gold, not only for me,
But for
Every
Family
I help
And
For
You

Jonathan Shen
Grade 10, Acalanes High School, Alameda County
Mrs. Challacombe, Classroom Teacher
Tureeda Mikell, Poet-Teacher

The Eyes of My Uncle's Face

My uncle is a study of the season
That opens out the sky winds
That blows the trees back and forth
His body is like a buffalo
Running with eagles and hawks
His eyes are brown like tree bark
His eyebrows are grey and black
Like snow falling from a dark sky
His skin is the light brown sand
Calling to him at the beach
When my uncle is happy
He turns into a red rose
Blooming from a bud
When he gets mad
It's thunder roaring from the sky
My uncle is like dolphins
Jumping from the ocean
to see the mountains
When my uncle laughs
He is a hawk lifting me from the ground
And carrying me to see the eagle
That talks to him and tells him what is wrong
When I look at him
He's an eagle flying over me
My uncle is a buffalo that runs wild
Hides from the hunter

Katrina Azbill
Grade 12, South Coast Continuation High School
Robert Wausen, Classroom Teacher
Blake More, Poet-Teacher

Jackhammer Hands

My dad's hands
wrinkled raisins
rougher than a bully's bite
a rock trying to scratch you.

When he washes his hands
they feel soft
like a swallow's feather
or a bunny's back.

His hands work hard
like jackhammers
breaking up the sidewalk.

Pedro Cardenos
Grade 4, Las Palmas, San Diego County
Catherine Pfizenmaier, Classroom Teacher
Johnnierenee Nelson, Poet-Teacher

Afghani Volcano

I come from Afghanistan
I come from a country
where everyone worries about war

A place where hunger
drought, sickness and death
are an everyday thing
— like brushing your teeth

a place where people
do not think about how
they look or what's in style
but how to make enough money
and if they'll survive until tomorrow.

Sometimes I feel like an erupting volcano
burning everything in its path
angry at people's selfishness
a wildfire burning until nothing's left to burn
yet sometimes I feel calm
a stream on a sunny day.

My life is like a kaleidoscope
not knowing what color, shape, or size
the next picture will be.

Edrees Nassir
Grade 7, The Charter School of San Diego, San Diego County
Samaiyah Vedder, Classroom Teacher
Johnnierenee Nelson, Poet-Teacher

Hope

Hope is a wise monk
meditating on a clear silent hill
bald and peaceful, seeking
answers, asking himself
many questions, wanting
an answer to stopping wars.

John Gregario
Grade 6, John Muir Middle School, Alameda County
Judy Rubin, Classroom Teacher
Kristin Palm, Poet-Teacher

My Grandfather's Eyes

My grandfather's eyes
    were the first thing people looked at.
My grandfather's eyes
    were what my grandmother loved about him.
My grandfather's eyes
    were big blue balls jumping.
My grandfather's eyes
    always looked at his six kids
    when they needed help.
My grandfather's eyes
    always looked at me
    ever since I was born
I would always smile
    like the half of the moon.
My grandfather's eyes
    sparkled like the stars
    on a warm night.

My grandfather's eyelids
    barely opened
    always told me when he felt bad or sick.
My grandfather's eyes
    were the last thing I looked at
    before he passed away.

Yanira Ramirez
Grade 6, John Muir Middle School, Alameda County
Judy Rubin, Classroom Teacher
Kristin Palm, Poet-Teacher

My Own World

I sit in my own room
sit sit sit
there there there
I sit
I sit there
with nothing to do
sit sit sit
there there there
I sit
I sit there
But
But not only there
but here
in my own world
Now you know a piece of my world
Now that you know
a piece of my world
now I can show you
the next door
walk through
climb in
buckle up
enjoy the ride
it's fast and interesting
"Now turning, left side"
Here is funville
Here we stop
Here is Jasmin's castle
where I drop you off
Now explore this neverending land
Do a little spin
and a little twirl
Now you are a piece of my world

Jasmin John
Grade 6, John Muir Middle School, Alameda County
Judy Rubin, Classroom Teacher
Kristin Palm, Poet-Teacher

My House

My house is a cage separating me
From the surrounding world.

My door is a slate of ice
Shielding me from harm.

My window is a fallen
Crescent moon resting
On a periwinkle sky.

My room is a snow
white cloud surrounded by four
imprisoning walls.

My yard is an open
Grassland in the
Middle of a tropical
Rainforest with exotic
Plants and gigantic
Waterfalls scattered
All around

I am a warm latté
On a cold winter day.

Holly Dolezal
Grade 5, C.L. Smith Elementary School, San Luis Obispo County
Patricia Foote, Classroom Teacher
Candi Pemberton, Poet-Teacher

The River and the Rain

Dear River Krka,
>How are the levels of your shores?
>I have heard you are running high.
>How are the fishermen faring this fall?
>I have heard you aren't being too generous.
>How is the temperature of your water?
>I have heard you are too cold for swimming.
>How wild are your currents?
>I have heard you have become a boating hazard.
>How is your great king of fish?
>I have heard a young American brag of sighting him.
>>Sincerely,
>>Rain Fall

Dear Rain Fall,
>Please stop sending water,
>It has caused more shores to overflow.
>Some of my friends in California are thirsty,
>They need the water more than I.
>I am punishing fishermen this year,
>The past few, they have over fished.
>The icy water is mostly your fault,
>Your mountain rains have filled me with freezing water.
>Your constant storms are also responsible for the raging water,
>Please stop, the currents are becoming a danger to everyone.
>My king has remained unseen since the American boy,
>He was the first and last to witness him.
>>Sincerely,
>>River Krka

Alex Moreland
Grade 9, Morro Bay High School, San Luis Obispo County
Bruce Badrigian, Classroom Teacher
Candi Pemberton, Poet-Teacher

Hope

You are Hope with a tail
of the sun. Your feet like the
light within, wishing for the
stone to vanish so you can be
set free. Just standing on thin
air like a wheat stalk in the
fenced up field. Your heart
is pounding like star, like sticks
flying through the air. You still
escape, but only because you're
Hope, I, I believe in you.

Morgan Riegert
Grade 6, West Side School
Scott Reid, Poet-Teacher

Hate And A Little Love

Hate is a black hole
Sucking people in
Not letting them out
Trapping them
Blocking them in brick walls
Like people in jail.

Hate is the scarlet devil
Tempting you
Spearing you with his pitchfork
Pulling you down to hell
Boiling you in his pot
Not letting you out.

Hate is black like a
Dark shadow of the night
Hate is all around us
It hurts with red anger
Hate is a strong sadness
Hate is ugly
Crushing people's souls
Shattering them
Fighting against love.

Love is God
Lending an arm
Picking you up
Holding you tight in strong arms
Not letting you go
Love is in you, in your heart.

Evan Muscat
Grade 5, St. Rita's School, Marin County
Susan Pence and Claudia Silva, Classroom Teachers
Michele Rivers, Poet-Teacher

Thoughts on Memories and Sadness

I want to live with all my memories,
Even if they're sad,
Even if they only hurt me,
Even if they're memories
I'd somehow rather forget.
If I keep trying,
Without running away,
If I keep trying, then someday
I'll be strong enough that
Those memories can't defeat me.
I believe that.
I want to believe there is no
Memory that is okay to forget.
I want to take every one of my memories
And hold them in my heart.
Because someday,
I'll overcome the pain
And have precious memories.

Sadness is a cold mist that surrounds me
And follows every move.
It pulls me down,
When I look up,
The only things there are ice-cold hands,
But they can't help.
I visit dark cold space,
No light.
Loneliness covers like a blanket of needles.
Then sadness and anger come and
Feed on my last hopes and dreams,
Until none are left.
The only way to escape
Is for love to come and grab my hand.

The pull back to life.

Kayla Hagstrom
Grade 6, Mill Valley Middle School, Marin County
Narahya Jolly, Classroom Teacher
Michele Rivers, Poet-Teacher

This Is the Blues

The Blues goes in my heart shakin' in the night.
The Jazz is the power of the music in the Blues.
The music is so interesting. The Blues is the
Jazz. I can feel the Jazz kickin' my head of the
music. I focus on Blues in my heart. The guitar
is the Blues of the music that I hear in
my heart. The colors of Blues are the people in
the city. I can feel the Blues goin' in my
head. The Jazz is the guitar.

Renessa Soriano
Grade 2, Longfellow Elementary, San Francisco County
Sandy Leong, Classroom Teacher
Sarah Rosenthal, Poet-Teacher

My Skin

Skin is a color
    it's a color of a dress
    who cares if it's dark
    who cares if it's as light as snow
It's no reason for slavery
At all no more
    no more at all
    it's skin a color
    no reason to cry
It's skin everyone has it
    even I

Jenessa Sabugo
Grade 3, Guadalupe Elementary, San Francisco County
Karleen Tindall, Classroom Teacher
Sarah Rosenthal, Poet-Teacher

Brother Who

When I'm bored my brother digs in me.
It makes me as bright as a lamp.
He is the sun and moon.
When he is sick I feel like the letter O.
I can't open my lips at all a peep.
He plays with me like winter and summer
take turns.
His hair is like the orange leaves in fall
floating to the ground.
His playful actions make me bright
as the sun.
When there's darkness in the sky his is
the sun.
I am the moon.

Anson Cheng
Grade 2, Palo Verde Elementary, Santa Clara County
Keri Garcia, Classroom Teacher
Sarah Rosenthal, Poet-Teacher

Depression

It comes creeping in the shadows.
You know it's there, rocking back and forth on its toes,
waiting to engulf you and drag you down.
You know it's there, waiting, watching,
staring you down, boring holes in you
with its eyes.
You know it's there. Inevitable, unsuffering madness:
chaos that doesn't cease,
a never-ending cycle.
The nightmare comes true.

He slashes at you, cuts that run deep
immense pain
a never-ending cycle.
His hands grab your throat.
No breathing, no seeing, no more being.
The nightmare comes true.

Courtney Adams
Grade 11, Phoenix School, Ventura County
Elizabeth Griffith, Classroom Teacher
Shelley Savren, Poet-Teacher

Untitled

Loneliness is cold with no blanket.
It has shining brown eyes
from all the tears inside.
It breathes deep breaths in and out.
The air is cool as it chills the inside
from the fingertips to the belly button
to the toe nails. Loneliness has no heart.
It has no soul. It has no love.
It probably feels like it has no friends,
no family. It feels like it has no purpose
as its hands reach for someone
when there's no one there.
It wants love, that's it,
to feel the warmth of someone there.
It is always there waiting, watching,
and afraid, afraid that no one will be there.
Now it looks like this:
dark skin, curly hair, long legs, reaching arms.
Wow! Loneliness looks just like me!

Diandra Friends
Grade 11, Phoenix School, Ventura County
Elizabeth Griffith, Classroom Teacher
Shelly Savren, Poet-Teacher

Evan

He rests on a couch by a wall,
his drink in his hand. He chuckles obnoxiously.
Studded denim, tight jeans, and a black eye.
They make him look somewhat ridiculous.
He reminds me of Sid Vicious;
his hair is poofy and he always sneers.
What a dirty, crusty rockstar.
He is making his guitar sound like a bulldozer,
for he has been drinking all day.
So skinny, it's like he has an eating disorder.
The van is nearly dead.
I miss the scumbag.

Andy Renshaw
Grade 12, Phoenix School, Ventura County
Mark Haug, Classroom Teacher
Shelley Savren, Poet-Teacher

Freedom

The strangest thing is freedom

It looks like blood or maybe guts

It sounds like *bam bam*, a shot from an AK-47

It feels just like a soldier's wound getting infected

It smells like gun powder

It tastes like a hostage's head

That's funny, our free will seems just like death

Soledad Jean-Pierre
Grade 7, Davidson Middle School, Marin County
Mark Wallace, Classroom Teacher
Prartho Sereno, Poet-Teacher

My Hands

Hands — they're dangling
over the world, putting a new light bulb
in the stars. Squeezing the rain
out of the clouds. Painting a rainbow.
They're worms, crawling down a table.
Or catching a shooting star.
Pinching the sparkling winter snow,
now and then, letting it go.
Hands — they thrust through the air,
just to catch a falling leaf.
Wrinkles all around,
making dips in the world.
When water is in my hands,
it is like the Pacific Ocean
on a calm sunny day.
My fingers strum the Milky Way,
making a soft sweet sound
the world can hear.

Lena Felton
Grade 4, Neil Cummins School, Marin County
Linnea O'Brien, Classroom Teacher
Prartho Sereno, Poet-Teacher

The Coming

Each Drop of Mamma's Candle
Sends the Coming of Spring

Each Flower Sister Picks
Sends the Coming of Summer

Each Bushel of Grain Pappa Harvests
Sends the Coming of Fall

Each Halloween Costume Grandmother Brings
Sends the Coming of Winter

Here I sit Sewing a Quilt
Looking out at the White Winter World
Each Stitch I Make SENDS the
coming of SPRING.

Nina Rondoni
Grade 5, Jefferson School, San Francisco County
Loret Peterson, Classroom Teacher
Susan Herron Sibbet, Poet-Teacher

From Summer to Fall

I can hear the maroon leaves
Crunching beneath my feet
As I watch the mahogany tree trunks
Squeeze together and shed.
Suddenly a breeze comes
And I see the leaves blowing
Running into each other
Like waves crashing down.
I watch the turquoise sky turn aqua
and feel the leaves rustling
as I run back to my house.
The summer door shuts on me
and I walk into Fall.

Cynthia Fernandez
Grade 5, San Diego County
Phyllis Collins, Classroom Teacher
Celia Sigmon, Poet-Teacher

What can't we share?

We are human.
We share milk to make us strong.
We are mammals.
We share the warm, bright sun.
We share the falling rain.
We share cold, frozen snow.
We share toys at our house.
We share toys at school.
We share clouds.
We share love.
We share pets.

We all need plants.
We all need the sun.
We all need food.
We all need water.
We all need cold milk and cooked vegetables.
We all need a brain to remember.
We are all people. We all have hearts.

Mrs. Smith's Kindergarten/First Grade Class
Grizzly Hill School, Nevada County
Will Staple, Poet-Teacher

Remember Me

Remember me,
the one you forgot to pick up at the park.
Remember me,
I was the one you laughed at when I fell off my bike.
Remember me,
I was the one you forgot to feed when I was a baby.
Remember me,
I was the one you left out in the cold rain.
Remember me,
I was the girl who asked for help on my homework.
You told me to go away!
Remember me?
I am the girl who is now grown up,
the one you don't remember.

Amy Jorgenson
Grade 8, Camptonville School, Yuba County
Mrs. Marovich, Classroom Teacher
Will Staple, Poet-Teacher

I am the Daughter of

I am the daughter of
A carpenter in China,
A builder, a soldier, housewives,
And ancestors of heaven

I come from the warm steamed
Rice served on an ancient
Bowl like winter snow,
Chinese sushi rolled up in

Seaweed like the sea's blue waves,
Steamed shrimp like a pink
Rose bed,
Golk jiy served on Lunar New Year's
Like a red envelope given to you.

My grandfather, who I never met
Was a builder, soldier, and carpenter.
The dwellings he built stand in China.
His skills were taught to my father.

My grandmother was a housewife and
Seamstress who took care of my father.

Even though they were poor,
They were still rich.
This is the name of the Wu family.

Anita Wu
Grade 5, West Portal Elementary School, San Francisco County
Marina Chiappellone, Classroom Teacher
Susan Terence, Poet-Teacher

State of Lies and Trust

Do you dream in red
like I do?
When your eyes are closed,
do the words stand out,
purple on grey?
There is a fig, burning, burning,
burning away . . .
I wouldn't let you drink my blood
if that's what would make you sing.
Sing for me now
let the fog wash over you.
Let the waves crawl over your toes
curious like rain
hungry like the dance.
The waves sneak up
begging you to sing
Is your sky blue?
Do mountains cut into your vision?
Like the teeth of a shark,
they gouge our flesh
trying to improve upon it.
Do you dream in red
like I do?
Can you see my words
painted purple
on the paper that is as
grey as the moon?
I tried to open up. I cut out my
heart and
offered you a bite.
By refusing it, you showed me your own
surrounded by thorny roses
and praying mantises by the dozen.

I bent down for a taste
oh, of that sweet looking
red and lavender heart.
I bent down for a taste
and your chest closed up
the hole was gone
with my greedy fingers still inside.
Do you dream in red
like I do?
Or is it blue
to match the hate in your eyes

Zachary Newman
Grade 12, Lincoln High School, San Francisco County
Danny Kim, Classroom Teacher
Susan Terence, Poet-Teacher

Ode to Lapis Lazuli

Your thick blue stripes scattered across your body
Like the morbid night
Pitch black with traces of distinguished blue clouds
Their cries of gray trickle down
And slowly move down your smooth coat
You lay on rich, soft soil
The moon and sky above you
To touch you is to feel the sadness of the clouds
To hold you is to sense the moon in my palm
Through you I encounter the colossal difference
of the heavens
The burning warmth of the stars
About to explode with rage in a misty fire
Through you I can feel the jagged rocks of Jupiter
Pushing against my feeble legs.
I touch the light breeze of wind as I circle around
the planets.
Slowly, I start to fall through the layers of sky
But land ever so lightly
The rain falls too, covering my entire shaky body
Yet my grip keeps firm
Your gracious presence is in my hand
And when I hold you
I hold all of the almighty heavens

Rita Volkovinskaya
Grade 9, Lowell High School, San Francisco County
Elizabeth Rogers, Classroom Teacher
Susan Terence, Poet-Teacher

Family

Pandas are my nature
Chinese, warm, and soft
Minorities in the forest
Of birds, tigers, deer.

The moon in full bloom
Full moon festival
Towering with light
Celebrated through mooncakes
Cut in half
Sweet brown dough
Around a golden-yellow yolk
Like the sun on the horizon.

Laughter and tasty, juicy smells
From the house full of people
Sardines packed in cans
On Chinese New Year's Eve
Small red envelopes bring good luck.

Chopped square tofu:
Mah-Jongg tiles,
Characters of peace and happiness
On the walls.

House washed
Sand by the shore
To clean away bad memories
Of the old year.

Pictures and Paintings
Fierce, respected dragons,
Beautiful venerable Phoenixes
Mystic authorities of the past:
Grandfathers and Grandmothers
Who will look after us in the future.

Children of the new:
Flowers still in bloom
Hear the familiar
Sounds of the language.

Parents around the table:
The merry-go-round in the park
Plates of minced beef, shrimp and walnuts,
Peking duck, abalone, *yeen who*,
Delicacies of the culture.
Yum Cha with ancient looking teapots.

Sunday mornings
Bamboo bowls filled with
Hot dim sums of pork, shrimp, green onions:
Chinese Sushi
Yellow chopsticks dabbing everywhere
Bamboos in the forest

Phoebe Tang
Grade 9, Lowell High School, San Francisco County
Svein Arber, Classroom Teacher
Susan Terence, Poet-Teacher

Ode To Bach

As jagged as a knife, the violin stroke
Upbeat, excited, thunderous
Yet smooth as a cool ocean breeze
Calming the soul.
Compliments from the bass
As perfect harmony forms.
Young, spirited sounds flow through the air.
Climatic productions pierce the mind
Controlling the being of the audience.
Tempo changes enlighten spirits.
Imagination sparks
Purity reformed
The heart of music portrayed.

Michael Villanueva
Grade 8, Marston Middle School, San Diego County
Carol Matori, Classroom Teacher
Gabriela Anaya Valdepeña, Poet-Teacher

We Celebrate
Our Poet Selves

Poet-Teacher Poems

Hair

When I was a child, relatives
fussed over my hair, ruffling its curls with
fingers and cooing in whispers.
I shrunk from the undeserved attention.
It was only hair! It wasn't me!

As a teen, I wanted to be blond.
Straight blond, down to here.
I attacked my hair like a soldier, pulled it,
ironed it, suffered curlers the size of pipes.

Then hippies, and I was in fashion.
A mane to shake and flout!
Thick, thick, thick and untamed.

As an adult, I tried every do.
Left parts. Right parts.
Ear length. Shoulder length.
Always curls and waves.
Never happy.

Now, my hair is thinning
and I long for that curly mass.
My hairdresser eyes the dull gray,
and I dye my locks, clutch at bottles and tubes.

I don't seem to have *my* hair anymore,
the hair I think of as covering my head.
On the playground.
On my first date.
When I brought the baby home from the hospital.

But what was that hair,
that look, so changeable,
impossible to recapture?

Cathy Barber
San Mateo County

This is How I Grew Up

With diffused light and secrets, dry leaves
piled under the Magnolia tree. Each week,
another Sunday. Tight sounds during church;
my life, twice as awake. Perceptions and words
lost to the wind. Only expressions remained —
sad, mad, happy — they reappear now
under different names. For each chance lost,
the heart has to work harder not to click itself shut.
These are the hymns of a childhood
I reinvent, as I learn to speak the invisible —
each day offering a new way to sing.

Karen Benke
Marin County

This Is Just To Say

(with a wave to William Carlos Williams)

Thank you for the peach pie
red gold, gooey, thick and crusty:
peaches carried heaped in a basket
up the hill from the tree we planted
seven years ago, watched over,
pruned, debugged, (harvested
one rock of a peach that first year)
and now its branches bent to the ground
on the uphill side, their burden of fuzzy
softening fruit almost more joy
than they can bear.
                    You rolled the dough
while I peeled fruit into a pail
my hands deep in the juice and pulp
my mouth smeared where I sucked
my fingers, my hair sticky on my forehead,
tiny fruit flies buzzing in the kitchen.

I helped you lift the flat crust with spatulas
and we laid it safely in the pan. You spiced
the golden bowl with cinnamon and other secrets,
criss-crossed the top with lattice crust,
and this morning, you gone off to school,
I cut a piece and served it on a small blue plate
with milk in blue cup.
                    I ate it slowly,
noticing every bite, watching the grasses move
as the breeze swept across the distant hills.

I've left the rest for you, sweet baker girl.
I'll be gone a few days,
but I'll be thinking of you
eating peach pie.

Gail Rudd Entrekin
Nevada County

A Kind Of Fountain

(read from the bottom up)

and pray he is still spouting light from his mouth as he goes.
ascended now as then, his words still splashing over me
I remember this child, twenty years past,
in my front yard gushing from warmed ground
Spring finally here, fountains of azaleas

to take a break.
praised his genius, told the teacher
put my arms around his slight shoulders
to the sun. Of course I rushed to his side
mounting words each a leaf in the reach
his tears a waterfall on his beautiful
we wanted he cried, pointing to me,
But she said we could write anyway
across the room.
that way. I heard the commotion from
The first-grade teacher said *No, not*
It was the first poem he wrote.
for instance from the roots up.
as a thing goes, a tree
the same direction
taught me to write
A child

Perie Longo
Santa Barbara County

Rejecting linear thinking   (a pantoum)

The circle within the circle I walk a-shimmer,
The sense it makes a matter of weather.
Listen to the snake steps this thinking demands,
Releasing the clouds that surround the heights.

The sense they make a matter of weather.
Children normally in the moment don't
Release clouds that surround the heights.
They depend on the tones within their homes.

Children normally in the moment can't
Understand: clocks scoop days in their hands.
They depend on the tones within their homes
To learn the spaces their steps must take.

At times I understand, clocks scoop days in their hands,
The circle within the circle I walk a-shimmer,
I sense the space my steps must take,
listen to the snaky walk my thinking demands.

Grace Marie Grafton
San Francisco County

My Mother's Face Reflects Winter Birds

Her nose in the kitchen, hopeful and pensive,
Eyes breezy, bare-armed branches, pale blue and glassy
but rippled like a white-capped ocean.
She has a school on her forehead,
lines like a paper filled with words
she never speaks, a wrinkled, bottomless pond
and dropped pebble, the nervous beige of a walnut shell.

Her chin is droopy and it itches; it pulls time backwards
and spins a cocoon that I withdraw into and am transformed.
When I emerge I am wearing her glasses, her mouth
has become my hair. Migrating birds carry me away.
It's a chariot of ice-blue silence they ride — my mother's silence
that screams everything I already know.

Scott Meltsner
Mendocino County

letters to a superior poet

"All poets are not created equal."
                    — stephan kessler

do you discern my choice of case
the letters small
like the millions of minds
other than yours
poetry minions who toil
in anonymous vastness
time seeping to ink
as we coax letters from the sun
filling the room with word scents
narcissus tinged sentences aloft
in an incense alive enough
to liberate beauty
from certain death

what makes you so certain
of your rank
how do you know one is less
another more
while you recline on cream leather
in your heaven of Coltrane and potted plants
others pace the streets of poetry
live the blue collar landscapes of expression
nights and days teeming with escalator images
the mad folly of our tenor solos
unhinged from your academic fences

we never loved the taste of postage stamps
the self adhesive ones don't help
because licking envelopes still leaves
a sour film on our tongues

what makes a poet superior?
his desire to rise above millions
or our willingness
to unfurl into pages of thought
splay them out
for no one, anyone
as long as it is love
supreme

Blake More
Mendocino County

The Principal

for Jon Cohee

His coffee cup waited
next to the keyboard. He'd wash
the dark rim when he returned.
Kid drawings decorated walls
with pointy-fingered suns, and fat-bellied
stick figures held the principal's hand.
Awards lined up so quietly
you could hear them breathe.

This was the man who planted trees
in the quad, chose poetry programs
over a copy machine,
stood outside his office
smiling like a giant teddy bear
every afternoon at dismissal.

The principal took off his glasses,
released his pants from suspenders,
unbuttoned his pin-striped shirt
and slipped arms through a hospital gown.
Kidney stones. He knew the routine.
Recovery. Lots of water.
Back to work midweek.

It was Friday. Poetry day.
The wind blew hot fierce air
that stuck to the backs of my legs
and shuffled my hair until the curls lay flat.
I jumped around the classrooms and kids wrote.
Nothing remained calm that afternoon.
Paper littered the school yard,
kids held books close and hurried home.

Teachers bent their strides toward the library.
We huddled, stuffing the room with silence,
all eyes intent on the superintendent.
Blood clot, he managed out.
I was first to leave.
I pressed my hands against my cheeks
to make certain they were real.
The wind carried the principal's smile away.

Shelley Savren
Ventura County

Three Haiku

<u>At the Rink</u>
Young girls spread velvet
     wings against a frozen sky
          and I fly with them

<u>Camp Almost Over</u>
Like the bites they show
     me each day, I already
          itch with missing them

<u>Autumn</u>
So small, the things we do:
     raking into piles miracles
          the trees have dropped.

Prartho Sereno
Marin County

Allen

Genuine Entity
Aren't you afraid of disintegrating?
Last free man who stormed complacency
to restore humanity to itself
Refugee in the war against yourself
on the verge of saying what voices
always seem about to say
Who gave in to desire so as to: not have desire
Who struggled to sketch the flow that Exists
Beat kind of face: inconceivable heartache
Magnificently blind abt. the flaws of lifetime friends
Embracer of social dissonance
Who was in touch with what one does not know
        that one knows
Heart sharp as a razor
    but open enough to be moved
        my lord of soft tender eyes
who never abandoned that wonderful
    ability to appear interested in everything
Who came to see the world as wholly holy
Who was enormously complimented
with the opportunity to turn poison
    into nectar, an adept
who could on an instant
    turn into someone else.

Will Staple
Nevada County

Pretty squirrel

Pretty squirrel have you come to my open window
To speak of peace or beg for my baguette?
Have you come, perhaps, to ask which way the wind blows?
Or could you have the troubles to forget

That I do? — sitting at dawn in my ragged gown
Crying in my coffee and burdening the jelly
With one true friend, forever in the ground.
Tell me, Dear Squirrel, what has become of Nelly?

Where do beloved creatures go? For I
Wouldn't give two cents for a full heaven without him.
Is there a simple place in the vast, great sky
For my pet's quiet star? — which sadly dimmed

While I was off to teach the little poets
To love all creatures; and now you poke your nose
Toward my tattered heart and try to sew it.
Oh squirrel, I fear this wound will never close.

Ardilla bonita

¿Ardilla bonita, has venido a mi ventana
Para hablar de la paz o rogar por mi bolillo?
¿Has venido, quizás, a preguntar de qué lado sopla el viento?
¿O puede ser que estas triste como yo? —

Sentada al alba en mi camisón raído
Molestando la jalea, llorando en mi café
Por un amigo verdadero que nunca despertó.
¿Querida Ardilla, qué ha sido de Nelly?

¿A dónde van amadas criaturas? Yo no daría
Un quinto por un cielo repleto sin él.
¿Hay un lugar sencillo en el gran cielo
Para la estrella tranquila de mi mascota? — que tristemente

Se desvaneció, mientras yo enseñaba a los pequeños poetas
A querer a toda criatura. Y ahora metes tu naricíta fria
Hacia mi corazón desgarrado, tratando de coserlo.
¡Ay ardilla, temo que esta herida nunca cerrará!

Gabriela Anaya Valdepeña
San Diego County

Essays and Lesson Plans

"Fire in the Belly 101:"
Teaching Poetry in an After-School Program

Claudia Jensen Dudley
San Francisco County

Dearest Muse,

I know it's your job to lead us, kicking and screaming, into the unknown, but sometimes I think teaching in an after-school poetry program tops it all. It's been ten years since you got me into this adventure, and it's time to send you a thank-you note. I remember how easy it sounded when I first heard about it. Teach one afternoon within walking distance of home. Have mornings to write. Go on doing school day teaching; it won't interfere. *A job made in heaven, right?*

Well, it's also your job to humble us. I hadn't yet heard about the burn-out and high turnover in after-school work when I walked into my first week of it. I had forty kids, two groups each, older and younger. One inexperienced teenage youth aide to help. In the older group, lots of boys itching to run, jump, scream, play basketball, throw stuff — anything but write. The younger group wanted all of the above and *also* needed massive individual help. Over the next weeks, lessons which had worked in four years of school day teaching now bombed royally. I came home from school feeling drained and hopeless. And you, dear Muse, were nowhere in sight.

There's at least one night in every poet-teacher's soul, and I think that was my first. Making poetry in the afternoon: isn't that an oxymoron? What adult poet expects to write immediately after her day job? Surely, dear Muse, you were laughing fiendishly. But one day around Thanksgiving, you sent the magic words: *"You've got to tame the boys."* A sexist epiphany, true, but these words changed my life. An idea unfolded; Why not take stories from the Norse, the mythic poem *Edda*, and tell them to the kids?

Replete with machismo, they had everything dear to boys' hearts: action, trolls, giants, one-eyed Odin, hammer-wielding Thor, and a world-ending battle at the end. I had the beautiful d'Aulaire book of Norse myths at home. Why not win the kids to poetry as Scherazade won back her life — story by story?

And so, dear Muse, a new adventure began, thanks as always to you. Yes, it was lots of work up front (I handwrote every story in my own words), but once written out, a story was mine to keep. I told the stories accompanied by a small children's harp. I made lessons simple and direct. The stories opened up thoughtful new vistas and gave classic teaching lessons new meaning. What emerged were lessons about magic powers, the four elements (water, fire, air, earth), time, secret places, dreams, beauty/ugliness, courage, the Sun, and so on.

And so dearest Muse, you came to help. I dropped purist ideals, allowed for one-line poems, took dictation whenever a kid, even an older one, was stuck. Poetry began to take off. You visited us all the time. After the Norse cycle came the *Mahabharata* from India, then cycles from the Greek, Arthurian, Celtic, Chinese, Tibetan, and Egyptian traditions, plus many individual stories.

I now start each class with closed eyes and twelve deep breaths — of the sky, the desert, the stars — whatever calms the afternoon beast in us all. I've found it best to alternate stories and "story" poetry with other kinds of lessons, emphasizing word games, hands-on and the absurd. I feel stories are sacred and should never become routine. And I tell the kids they must pay me for stories "with $500,000 worth of silence" and the poems that follow.

So, dear Muse, why do I love this job, now three afternoons a week, which still takes all the belly fire I can muster? Well, because it's like riding waves in all weather, or dancing to music that's always new. It keeps your mind nimble and your psychic joints flexible. And sometimes it seems almost as heroic (meaning harrowing) as any myth in the books. Kids' afternoon fatigue and fidgets always play into it. But if I stay rooted to the earth and my fellow staff members, all of us holding patience, humor and self-respect close at hand, the magic can happen. We get to crawl inside stories and live there. We get to voyage with the kids through human drama of every kind. And poems of depth and contemplation rise up amidst the many zany ones. At the same time, the kids never let you forget what "works" after school: absurdity, irreverence, R&R, laughter, hyperbole, fun. And over and over again, they say they love the stories.

I will bring this to a close, dear Muse, with a memory of two moments that could only happen in an after-school program. The first was long ago in that first class when Casey, a lively, intractable first grader, assured me, "We don't like you but we like your stories." That's when I knew the fever had turned, so to speak. Years later I was sitting at dusk on a bench in the schoolyard with Victoria, a fifth grader. We watched in silence as the sky darkened to a clear, starry blue, rare in our neighborhood. One of us (I honestly don't remember which) said, *"Isn't it strange how you have to use your imagination to get to the truth?"* In that rare dusk moment, an immutable insight had emerged, both old and new. For that and for hundreds of other moments — rewarding, soul-wrenching, tooth-pulling or just plain happy — I offer all my gratitude, dearest Muse. And yes, come Tuesday afternoon, I *will* jump back into the fire.

Sample poems from the Richmond District After-School Collaborative, San Francisco:

Recipe 4 Angry Teachers

3 cups of trouble makers
Remove listening ears
Add wrong homework & bad temper
Add coffee with cream
Stir carefully & serve to teachers

Tyler Kung
Grade 4

I am a person listening to the air. I am dead but I am being born once more. I am flying with mother eagle again.
I am someone that dies and comes back to life.
I am the person that haunts every dark corner in every street.
I was the water that flooded the world when Noah
made the boat of the seas. I am the light in the sky.
I walked with god in space when he first appeared.
I was a book for the greatest sorcerer.

Oliver Feeney
Grade 3

The Spiral Conspiracy

Terri Glass
Marin County

Shapes in nature have always fascinated me so I decided to create a lesson plan around my favorite shape which is the spiral. The spiral is an intriguing form because it is repeated throughout nature from the smallest microscopic spirochete to the great cosmic galaxy nebula. It is even in our DNA molecule. It is the most versatile pattern in nature growing from the center outward through a cautious route of expansion and exploration.

In art, spirals represent growth and change (see Angeles Arrien's book, *The Signs of Life*). In science, spirals represent an efficient use of space. If you look at a chambered nautilus shell, you find a mathematical precision of growth known as the Fibonacci series. Knowing these two perspectives, I was curious what children would reveal about themselves if they became a spiral.

I begin this lesson brainstorming with the students where they see spirals in nature and list them on the board. Tornadoes, whirlpools, pinecones, sunflowers, seashells, fiddlehead ferns and a spider's web are just a few of the forms that children will think of. Then I read a couple of poems that represent this shape. Mary Oliver has a beautiful poem, *The Sunflowers* (from the book *Dreamwork*, pg. 88), or Rainer Maria Rilke's *I live my life in growing orbits* (from the *Selected Poems of Rainer Maria Rilke* translated by Robert Bly, pg. 12). Then I read one of my poems, *Spiraling*.

Spiraling

I'm tight
held within the closet of my heart.
I want to burst free free FREE
and spin around and around
'til I drop on top of the grass
and see the blue sky spinning,
the clouds cart-wheeling
and the birds whirling into each other

like Escher's design
while the great eddies
of the nearby rivers
sing to the salmon
as they are pulled
into the vortex of whirlpools
tingling their silver scales.
Meanwhile the snails on land
decide to roll away
like the runaway pancake.

Terri Glass

Next I have the children choose one type of spiral and I have them
close their eyes for a visualization where I guide them and ask the
following questions:

1. Imagine being inside the whorl of a spiral.
2. You begin compacted from the center and grow outward in an
    ever-expanding circle.
3. What does it feel like to begin curled up and then radiate out?
4. What color are you?
5. What do you hear as you grow in spiral fashion?
6. What does it feel like growing into larger orbits?

Immediately, I have the children begin writing. I encourage them
to use sensory detail and vivid verbs describing their shape and action.
Creating a list of verbs on the board can be helpful. Some children will
concentrate on one spiral; others may include many types of spirals in
their poems. It is even fun if they want to write their poem in the
shape of a spiral. Here are some sample poems from this lesson from
children of West Marin School, Pt. Reyes Station.

Inside a Sunflower

Inside the sunflower, I'm in a swirl
of many different colors.
It sounds like the bees buzzing.
It feels like walking on clouds.
I can even taste the sweet nectar.
I feel my feet drop.
I am curving and going up
Then I find myself on the head
of my sunflower.
I see the sun.
I feel free as a bird
flying through the sky.

Paulita Gonzalez
Grade 5

Shell

I'm a shell. I watch the waves,
doing a spiral all day and everyday,
same thing over and over,
blue then white.
It's so tempting to go in the waves,
but I don't have legs.
I wish somebody would pick me up
and throw me in the waves,
throw me as far as they can.

Nick Waldrup
Grade 6

Spiral

Spiral,
the shape of life,
how it makes you
dizzy.
A snake in its den
curled up to sleep
the winter away,
a hermit crab
inside his spiraling home,
a spiraling vine
is a monkey's way of life
around.
We all have
a spiral of
life.
Just some
of us
don't know
what it is.

Brian Hollern
Grade 6

Since poetry is a recognition of patterns of sound and image, combining it with the recognition of patterns in nature can be a powerful tool of understanding ourselves. If we align ourselves with the design of nature, a great wisdom can unfold.

Listening to Echoes: Remembering Gerry Grace

Karen Lewis
Mendocino County

In early January, driving to my first workshop at Dana Gray Elementary, I detoured into the Albion Post Office to mail some manuscripts. The wall held an exhibit of paintings, recent work by the late poet-teacher Gerry Grace. It was fitting that Gerry's paintings calmed me; part of her spirit soared with me to school. During that day, Gerry shadowed my footsteps throughout the hallways that she, too, once visited as a poet-in-residence.

Before the first class, one teacher took me aside to share a poem that Gerry had written in her classroom last spring. This poem seems emblematic of the truth and grace that Gerry brought to her students. No topic is too difficult to write about. All emotions are welcome in the classroom of the imagination.

Death
for my Mother

She did not leave
in roaring flames
More like wisps of some
small bits of charred wood
I had been away
Not at home in seven years
When I arrived
a coolness throughout the house
Silence
Only
Ashes

Gerry Grace

Introducing myself to the third graders that day, I mentioned that I was filling in for another poet-teacher, a friend who had recently died, Gerry Grace.

At the recess break, a young girl came up to me and asked, "You know that part I wrote about what I see in the clouds? It's really my dad."

I looked at her, gave her a moment of silence, then responded, "Do you mean that your poem is about your dad who died?"

She nodded.

"Poetry can be a good way to share these feelings," I affirmed.

A month later, I was substitute teaching in another school where Gerry had led visual arts workshops. The classroom teacher, Gail, more than many, always brings art to her students each year. I expected to find a void, the walls bare of self-portraits and "dreamscapes" that Gerry encouraged the students to create. However, in the teacher's planner, I noticed Gail's compilation of student memories of Gerry. "She always had really fun or cool earrings." "She taught me to draw from the inside, to draw my feelings." "She taught me to draw my dreams." "BIG RULE #1 Nothing is a mistake." Pretty powerful memories from fourth graders. The student wrote BIG RULE in all caps, just as you read it here. There is no mistake that Gerry's paintings called to me to school that day. No mistake that she wrote of death, painted dreams, played with words, wore remarkable earrings — inspired grace.

So, what does this all mean? That we do not really die? That our footsteps in the classroom echo beyond hours spent there? Yes, today, we hold the incredible privilege of touching young writers with words, with hope, and with the truth born of difficult emotions and complex realities. When we encourage the world of writing, we celebrate our true selves, and nurture young poets to discover their imaginative powers; to heal the fragile self, to imagine and to create more perfect worlds. Thank you, Gerry.

Tomatoes Invade the Classroom and the Snail Leaves Its Mark . . .

Susan Terence
San Francisco County

To write impassioned poetry of the fruits of the earth, students planted seeds in the cool mud in early fall and harvested and tasted the fruits of their labor in late winter.

Poetry was at the heart of the collaborative project for over two hundred third to fifth graders at Ulloa Elementary School in San Francisco. Adult collaborators included two school gardening teachers, one school district nutritionist, one CPITS poet-teacher, and six participating teachers including third grade teacher, Edna Kwan, who facilitated the S.F. Ed. Fund grant for the project.*

In October and November students examined the parts of a corn plant before reading the Navajo poem: *"My great corn plants,/Among them I walk,/I speak to them,/They hold out their hands to me"* and the Tohono O'odham poem, *"Blue evening falls/Blue evening falls./Nearby in every direction/It sets the corn tassels trembling."*

Our in-class "Thanksgiving" involved reading several of Chilean poet Pablo Neruda's odes to foods and seasons and then tasting several fruits and vegetables native to the Americas. Before writing their own ardent odes, students sampled bitter, raw red cranberries; pale, watery, crunchy jicama; sweet crispy green peppers; pale green creamy avocado; lush red orange persimmons; large juicy red tomatoes; spongy white, yellow, and green summer squash; and tangy grapes and strawberries. (The book *Chiles to Chocolate: Food the Americas Gave the World* from the University of Arizona press, 1992, also lists allspice, lima and tepary beans, blackberries, black raspberries, blueberries, chocolate, cocoa, chili pepper, maize, tomatillos, pineapples, pumpkins and sweet potatoes as among the foods native to the Americas.) We reminded students to create metaphors comparing the color, shape, texture and aroma of their foods to landscapes, jewels, flowers, animals, celestial objects before tasting their fruit or vegetable treasure. Suggested beginnings to their food odes were: "Green of. . . .", "Red as a _____," "(Name of fruit or vegetable), you are a _____." We included a list of adjectives describing tastes and textures (such as *"sweet, tangy, juicy, sour, creamy, minty, bitter, warm, wet, crunchy, crusty, bumpy, rough, gritty, spiky, silky, glassy, thorny, spiny*) and also asked students to consider an emotion or behavior they'd associate with each food (*the lonely zucchini, the angry cranberry, the impish jicama*).

The exercise was a success not only in generating exciting and expressive poetry by the students, but in introducing them to foods they'd never tasted. None had ever tasted raw cranberries; few had even heard of jicama (but liked it once they tried it); most were intrigued by the raw zucchini and summer squash; and they were in rapture over the ripe persimmon.

The bountiful winter rains guaranteed the proliferation of the students' lettuce, greens, radishes and other root crops. The school gardening teacher harvested salad greens and radishes for a late winter salad bar, and grant facilitator Edna Kwan and SFUSD school health programs nutritionist Saeeda Hafiz supplemented the school's harvest with additional vegetables and toppings to provide a free salad bar lunch to 225 third–fifth graders. The students were ecstatic — most wanted seconds.

The next day, armed with plates filled with more of their garden vegetables — the otherworldly kohlrabi; blood red radishes; purple and green oakleaf lettuce; white flowering arugula; massive nasturtium leaves; and green veiled parsley — along with a new selection of Neruda's odes and other model poems, students composed "Odes to their Salad Bar Vegetables."

I asked students to recite Neruda's passionate "Ode to the Plum" as if they were over-eager actors at an audition. They happily complied, placing their hands over their heart as they read: *"The earth, the sun, the snow/ . . . Oh kiss/of the mouth on the plum/teeth and lips full of fragrant amber . . ."* While reading, students joyously lifted imaginary glasses in the air to complete the Neruda poem: *"I drink and toast to life/in your honor/whoever you are, wherever you go/I don't know who you are/but I leave in your heart a plum . . ."* I suggested they read aloud Neruda's "Ode to Tomatoes" as if they were narrating a "spaghetti western." *"The street filled with tomatoes/midday summer light is halved like a tomato, its juice/runs through the streets/ . . . In December, the tomato invades the kitchen . . ."*

Wallace Stevens' "Thirteen Way of Looking at a Blackbird" not only served as the model for several students' poems, but also inspired our class group poems about the freshly picked spiky and leafy kohl-rabi: "*1. A flying green Giants' baseball with twenty arms sailing into McCovey's Cove 2. The green earth in its lonely orbit . . .*"

A surprising element in the writing was the inclusion of tenacious and inquisitive brown snails that accompanied the extra greens I'd picked from my home garden for the class writing exercise. Students vied for the honor of having a snail slowly gnaw its way through the greens on their table, so I periodically carried the snails on their own leafy thrones of lettuce from table to table. The Aztec poem that begins, "What is my song?/My song is a piece of jade . . ." inspired Ulloa third grader Michael Lam (in Ms. Sharon Blean's class) in his poem about the snail at his table: "*What is my song?/My song is a brown snail/It is my little gold ring/It is my black eye/it is my green nail/It is my little black shell.*"

Students were delighted to grow and taste their own vegetables; to read Pablo Neruda's sumptuous odes to vegetables and fruits; to learn the history and life cycle of many foods of the Americas; and to write poems about the fruits of their labors.

Ulloa third grader Gerianna Geminiano's poem (from Edna Kwan's class) is a fitting tribute to the impact of the project:

> The orange carrot is all that's left of memory.
> The green lettuce is the last of the heart.
> The smooth snail's skin is my eyes.
> The purple radish is my family.
> The light green arugula is my grandfather's treasure.
> The yellow and the orange is part of my family.
> The orange is my grandmother's treasure.
> The roots of the lettuce are my growth chart.

* Notes on the collaborators: Ulloa gardening teachers, John Kuroda and Sarah Hill were funded by the Ulloa Childcare Center and had students plant seeds kindly donated by Pinetree Garden Seeds in New Gloucester, Maine. Nutritionist Saeeda Hafiz worked at Ulloa under a grant through the SFUSD School Health Programs Department. Susan Terence, SF CPITS poet-teacher, received her funding for the project through the San Francisco Education Fund and the Ulloa PTA. Principal Carol Fong and poetry grant coordinator Edna Kwan facilitated the collaboration. Students' poems and family recipes were gathered into an anthology entitled *Recipes for Life*.

Baudelaire

Gabriela Anaya Valdepeña
San Diego County

Charles Baudelaire was the granddaddy of French Symbolism, a movement in poetry, which found parallels in the Impressionist and Postimpressionist movements of art and music. Symbolism introduced into French poetry an intense artistic focus on the everyday, and sometimes sordid, details of urban life, while at the same time maintaining a careful and minute attention to the craft of the verse. Symbolism, moreover, was less interested in "the thing" itself (see Wallace Stevens) than in "the thing" as a vehicle toward something that could never be explained directly in language. Symbolists were devoted to the will o' the wisp, the lingering dream that could not be recapitulated.

Baudelaire combined a mastery of craft with an accursed, rebellious spirit, embracing both the grotesque and the sublime. He explored extreme psychological states, moving against the current of propriety, in an attempt to confront the irrepressible shadow of death and blight. In doing so, he celebrated those who lived on the fringe of society, seeking to make art, somehow, out of the squalor of bohemian Paris.

In Baudelaire, the reader may find commiseration in a poet who does not judge our innermost thoughts. Teen poets relate to him because in Baudelaire they find themselves corroborated and exalted, and given freedom to explore their myriad selves with impunity. In creating their own Baudelairean poems, they can sublimate their angst, reconcile the paradoxes of the world, and make peace with the contradictions in their very being. Baudelaire's exquisite and carefully crafted verse allows us all to move beyond hypocrisy to experience beautiful and painful truths.

I have found that some of the best student poems are written in the excitement generated by the work of the best poetic models. I try to show how poets such as Baudelaire have inspired me so that students may learn how to inspire themselves. Usually, I read model poems such as Baudelaire's "Metamorphoses of the Vampire" out loud, then have a lively discussion, avoiding excessive exercises, lest they dissipate the energy. Then I re-read the poems, silently queue the adagios, dim the lights and let them write. The following student poem was written in response to this approach, and they do seem inspired by Baudelaire's intense confessional energy, linking paradoxical images in a rich network of rhythm and sound.

The Ascension, a lobotomy

I am the echo rising from the embers of ages.
I embody a note
Held like a breath.
Inhaling the dance of dust,
Amidst the snarls of instruments and implements,
I see the steam pulsing from eternity
In the fog of an ether dream.

Then the conductor raises his scalpel
And severs endless centimeters of memory
And sifts this whole history through a burlap hourglass
And cuts every question into unasked answers.

I have not lost consciousness; it was stolen from me.
Reading the runes of a past collapsed,
I will now know my memories by maps.

Matthew Vollgraff
Grade 12

Bibliography

Publication Opportunities

Before you send any work in, check the Writer's Guidelines, which are usually either on the website or inside the magazine. Pay attention to word count and any themes that might be requested. If a contest has a DEADLINE, make sure that your work arrives before deadline!

Send your best work and have a teacher, friend or parent check your manuscript for typos first. Use white paper, 8½" x 11" and black ink with a normal font Times 12 point. Follow the guidelines carefully. For example, type your name and page number on each page, unless requested NOT to — sometimes contests want "blind" manuscripts with a separate cover sheet that has your title listed on it.

Every submission needs a cover letter and a SASE (self-addressed-stamped-envelope) so that the publisher can reply to your submission. Don't be discouraged if at first you don't succeed. Every rejection slip brings you one step closer to being published. Make sure to keep copies of any work that you submit. When your work is published, you will receive a copy of the issue, and sometimes payment, too. Keep copies or "clips" of all your published work. Best of luck in your efforts!

Updated by Karen Lewis, May 2005.

Hanging Loose magazine has published high school writers in every issue, and they have put together several anthologies of high school writing: Hanging Loose Press, 231 Wyckoff Street, Brooklyn, NY 11217. **www.hangingloosepress.com.**

Imagine, a magazine for students 12–18 years publishes stories, poems, essays, and book reviews. Editor, CTY/Imagine, Johns Hopkins University, 3400 N. Charles Street, Baltimore, MD 21218. Or visit them on the web at **www.jhu.edu/gift/imagine/guidelines**. Also offers a variety of academic opportunities.

Merlyn's Pen: An annual publication of essays, stories, and poems by students in grades 6–12. Check out at **www.merlynspen.com.** Large archive of resources for writers and teachers.

New Moon: The Magazine for Girls and their Dreams, for girls age 8-14. Check out their website and guidelines before submitting work. **www.newmoon.org.** New Moon, 34 East Superior Street #200, Duluth, MN 55802.

River of Words sponsors an annual poetry and art contest for students **www.riverofwords.org.**

Skipping Stones features multi-cultural, international perspective. Poetry, personal-experience essays, and short stories. **www.skippingstones.org.** Skipping Stones, P.O. Box 3939, Eugene, OR 97403.

Stone Soup: Publishes poems and stories by kids through age 13. **www.stonesoup.com.**

Scholastic has an annual competition for writers, photographers, and artist. For grades 7–12. Website has complete information on entries and examples of past award winners. **www.artandwriting.org.**

Teen Ink publishes poetry and short prose, on-line and in print. Read a sample before submitting your work. Information about workshops, college programs, and related writer resources. **www.teenink.com.**

Waging Peace. A wealth of peace resources, including poetry and essay contests. **www.wagingpeace.org.**

Writing Magazine, Weekly Reader, 200 First Stamford Place, Stamford, CT 06912. For grades 6–10. Editor Sandhya Nankani says, "we are always looking to publish student writing." Email her at **snankani@weeklyreader.com** for guidelines.

Other Poetry Resources, Online

Academy of American Poets. Find a poet, find a poem. **www.poets.org**.

Center for the Art of Translation promotes literature and translation. Home of **Poetry Inside Out**, a bilingual school-based program. Anthologies available. **www.catranslation.org**.

California Poets in the Schools, 1333 Balboa Street, San Francisco, CA 94118. (415) 221-4201. **www.cpits.org**. Places professional writers in classrooms throughout California.

Carnegie Library. Resources and literature for children and teens. **www.clpgh.org**.

Inner Spark summer program for students 8th–12th grades passionate about music, creative writing, dance, film, visual art, animation, or theatre. Find their website at **www.csssa.org**.

New York Public Library. Literary resources for students, writers, and teachers. **www.nypl.org**.

Oyate, 2702 Matthews Street, Berkeley, CA 94702. Native American Studies. Oyate is the Dakota name for people. **www.oyate.org**.

Poets & Writers is published bimonthly with interviews, publication opportunities, and links to other literary sites. **www.pw.org**.

San Francisco State University Poetry Archives. Wide range of video, audio, written work by living and historic poets. Diverse range of styles and voices. **www.sfsu.edu/~poetry/**.

Teachers & Writers Collaborative, 5 Union Square West, New York, NY 10003-3306. Publishes catalog of writing tools and offers comprehensive website with many literary links. **www.twc.org**.

Teaching Tolerance. Lesson plans, posters free to educators and students. **www.tolerance.org**.

Write Girl provides mentoring, creative writing workshops, performance and publication opportunities for teen girls in the Los Angeles region. Find them at **www.writegirl.org.**

Writers Corps, a project of the San Francisco Arts Commission, reaches out to young writers ages 6–14 in a variety of neighborhood and school centers. **www.writerscorps-sf.org.**

Youth Speaks. Written and spoken word in the San Francisco Bay Area. **www.youthspeaks.org.**

826 Valencia Street Project. In San Francisco's Mission District, writing programs for all age groups. Poetry, science fiction, experimental writing, bookmaking, tutoring. They welcome English language learners. Check it out at **www.826valencia.org.** In Los Angeles, find program details at **www.826la.org.**

Poetry Books Recommended for Students & Teachers

While compiling this bibliography, we've aimed for cultural and stylistic breadth, with an eye toward fine examples to enjoy and teach poetry across all age levels. — Karen Lewis, May 2005

Alarcón, Francisco W. *Iguanas in the Snow: Poems to Dream Together.* Bilingual. pre-K–4th.

Angelou, Maya. *Complete Collected Poems of Maya Angelou.*

Begay, Shonto. *Navaho: Visions and Voices Across the Mesa.*

Bierhorst, John, ed. *In the Trail of the Wind: American Indian Poems.* 2nd–up.

Bishop, Wendy. *Thirteen Ways of Looking for a Poem: A Guide to Writing Poetry.*

Brandeis, Gayle. *Fruitflesh: Seeds of Inspiration for Women Who Write.*

Clinton, Catherine. *I, Too, Sing America: Three Centuries of African American Poetry.*

Creech, Sharon. *Love that Dog.* Novel in free verse. 3rd–6th.

Foster, Tonya and Prevallet, Kristin, eds. *Third Mind: Creative Writing Through Visual Art.*

Franco, Betsy, ed. *You Hear Me: Poems by Teenaged Boys; Things I Have to Tell You.*

Gale, David, ed. *When the Rain Sings: Poems by Young Native Americans.*

Gilbert, Derrick I.M. (a.k.a. D-Knowledge) *Catch the Fire!!!*

Grant, James P., ed. *I Dream of Peace: Images of War by Children of Former Yugoslavia.*

Greenfield, Eloise. *In the Land of Words.* K–up.

Hamill, Sam, ed. *Crossing the Yellow River: Three Hundred Poems from the Chinese.* 4th–up.

Hass, Robert, ed. *Essential Haiku: Poet's Choice: Poems for Everyday Life.*

Hesse, Karen. *Aleutian Sparrow; Witness*; novels in free verse. 4th–7th.

Ho, Minfong. *Maples in the Mist: Children's Poems from the Tang Dynasty.* K–6th.

Holbrook, Sara, ed. *Walking on the Boundaries of Change.* Anthology. 5th–12th.

Hudson, Wade, ed. *Pass It On: African American Poetry for Children.* Pre-K–4th.

Hughes, Langston. *The Dream Keeper and Other Poems.* K–up.

Janeczko, Paul B. *Seeing the Blue Between: Advice & Inspiration for Young Poets.* 6th–10th.

Jordan, June. *Poetry for the People: A Revolutionary Blueprint.*

Koch, Kenneth. *Rose, Where Did You Get That Red? Teaching Great Poetry to Children.*

Marazán, Julio, ed. *Luna, Luna: Writing Ideas from Spanish, Latin American and Latino Lit.*

McClatchy, J.D., ed. *Vintage Book of Contemporary World Poetry.*

McEwen, Christian and Statman, Mark. *The Alphabet of the Trees: A Guide to Nature Writing.*

Milosz, Czeslaw, ed. *A Book of Luminous Things.* Anthology, international. 4th–up.

Myers, Walter Dean. *Harlem; Brown Angels.* Illustrated poems. K–5th.

Neruda, Pablo. *The Essential Neruda: Selected Poems.* Ed. Mark Eisner. Español and English.

Nolen, Jerdine. *Plantzilla.* K-up.

Nye, Naomi Shihab, ed. *The Space Between Our Footsteps; This Same Sky.* 4th–up.

Padgett, Ron, ed. *Handbook of Poetic Forms.* As essential as a dictionary!

Philip, Neil, ed. *War and the Pity of War.* 5th–up.

Pinsky, Robert, ed. *Americans' Favorite Poems: The Favorite Poem Project Anthology.*

Prelutsky, Jack, ed. *Random House Book of Poetry for Children.* K–5.

Rexroth, Kenneth, ed. *100 Poems from the Japanese.*

Rodriguez, Luis J. *Concrete River; Poems Across the Pavement.* YA.

Rosenberg, Liz. *The Invisible Ladder; Light-Gathering Poems; Earth-Shattering Poems.*

Sneve, Virginia Driving Hawk, ed. *Dancing Teepees: Poems of American Indian Youth.*

Sones, Sonya. *Stop Pretending; What My Mother Doesn't Know.* Novels in verse. YA.

Soto, Gary. *Neighborhood Odes.* 4th–up. *New & Selected Poems.* YA.

Wolff, Virginia Euwer. *Make Lemonade Trilogy.* Novels in narrative verse. 7th–12th.

Yep, Laurence. *American Dragons: Twenty-five Asian Voices.* YA.

CPITS Poet-Teachers

ALAMEDA COUNTY
Opal Palmer Adisa
Giovanna Capone
Janice De Ruiter
J. Ruth Gendler
Carmen Johnston
Tobey Kaplan
Lisa Klein
Lindsay Knisely
Alison Luterman
Tureeda Mikell
Margot Pepper
Alison Seevak
Mara Sheade
John Oliver Simon
Judith Tannenbaum
Alan Tinker

BUTTE & TEHAMA COUNTIES
Danielle Alexich
Joanne Allred
Heather Fisher
Marilyn Ringer
Susan Wooldridge

CONTRA COSTA COUNTY
Nicola Waldron
Laura Walker

HUMBOLDT COUNTY
Daryl Chinn
Daniel Zev Levinson
Jerry Martien

INYO & EAST SIERRA COUNTIES
Eva Poole-Gilson

LOS ANGELES COUNTY
Fernando Castro
Lori Davis
Tina Demirdjian
Virginia Haddad
Yvonne Mason
Jamie O'Halloran

Kirsten Ogden
Natalie Pace
Alice Pero
Wendy Person Fisher

MADERA COUNTY
Mary Lee Gowland

MARIN COUNTY
Lea Aschenas
Karen Benke
Duane BigEagle
Albert F. DeSilver
Sasha Eakle
Kathy Evans
Terri Glass
Robin Jacobson
Dana Lomax
Michele Rivers
Prartho Sereno

MENDOCINO COUNTY
Hannah Clapsadle
Lasara Firefox
Karen Lewis
Susan Maeder
Scott Meltsner
Blake More
Dan Roberts

NEVADA, PLACER & SIERRA COUNTIES
Thekla Clemens
Gail Entrekin
Molly Fisk
Lisa Gluskin
Christine Irving
Will Staple

ORANGE COUNTY
Steve Ramirez

RIVERSIDE COUNTY
Jo Scott Coe
Frances Ruhlen McConnel

SACRAMENTO COUNTY
Francisco Alarcón
Jo Ann Anglin
Marie Altman
Jason Cudahy
Jon Chris Olander

SAN DIEGO COUNTY
Francisco Bustos
Brandon Cesmat
Veronica Cunningham
Glory Foster
minerva (Gail Hawkins)
Jana Gardner
Georgette James
Paula Jones
Seretta Martin
Jill Moses
Johnnierenee Nelson
Celia Sigmon
Ross Joseph Talarico
Gabriela Anaya Valdepeña

SAN FRANCISCO COUNTY
Dan Bellm
Leslie Kirk Campbell
Tom Centollela
Tina Cervin
Sally Doyle
Claudia Dudley
Julie Gamberg
Karen Garman
Grace Grafton
Lewis Jordan
devorah major
Gail Newman
Carlos Ramirez
Irwin Rosen
Sarah Rosenthal
Susan Sibbet
Susan Terence

SAN LUIS OBISPO COUNTY
Jane Elsdon
Michael McLaughlin
Kevin Patrick Sullivan

SAN MATEO COUNTY
Cathy Barber
Jennifer Swanton Brown
Sarah Anne Cox
Antonio Facchino
John Fox
Mary Lee McNeal
Nancy Mohr
Emmanuel Williams

SANTA BARBARA COUNTY
Lois Klein
Christine Kravetz
Perie Longo
Teresa McNeil MacLean
Elizabeth Taylor-Schott

SANTA CRUZ COUNTY
Marty Campbell
Kimberley Nelson

SONOMA & NAPA COUNTIES
Molly Albracht
Arthur Dawson
Richard Denner
Claire Drucker
Terry Ehret
Jackie Hallerberg
Susan Kennedy
Luis Kong
Penelope La Montagne
Phyllis Meshulam
Gwynn O' Gara
Scott Reid

VENTURA COUNTY
Elijah Imlay
Lucia Lemieux
Richard Newsham
Shelley Savren

YOLO COUNTY
Eve West Bessier
Rae Gouirand
Kris McLeod
Andrea Ross
Allegra Silberstein
Martin Woodside

CALIFORNIA
POETS IN THE
SCHOOLS

About Us

We help students throughout California to recognize and celebrate their own creativity, intuition, and intellectual curiosity through the creative writing process. Our multi-cultural community of poet-teachers bring their experience and love for their craft into the classroom every school day.

California Poets in the Schools is the largest artist-in-residence program in the nation. We have been bringing our program to schools for over 40 years. Though we are not part of any one school district, we teach in public and private schools, juvenile halls, and hospital programs, and send over 170 poets into classrooms throughout California.

Our poet-teachers are professional, published writers who are trained in the art of teaching poetry to children. They are from diverse cultural and ethnic heritages and serve as living models of commitment to imaginative language and creativity.

We endeavor to make creative writing an integral part of the education of young people. We encourage young people to recognize, examine, and value culture, imagination, perception, and creativity, and help them foster an appreciation for self-expression.

We also share and affirm the cultural diversity of California by bringing poets and artists of color into the classroom and using multi-cultural materials in our lessons.

We hope you enjoy this anthology of our students' work.

California Poets in the Schools can be contacted at:
Phone: 415-221-4201
Toll Free: 1-877-274-8764
Email: info@cpits.org — Visit our Website: www.cpits.org

Please Join Us!

CALIFORNIA
POETS IN THE
SCHOOLS

There are many ways you can help us to: **Encourage** the creative writing, critical thinking, and self-esteem of our children, **Share** and affirm the diversity of California by ensuring that our schools bring culturally competent poets and multi-cultural materials into the classroom, and **Build** partnerships between schools, the community, poets and artists.

Please join CPITS at the highest level you can afford:

❑ $10,000 Angel

❑ $5,000 Laureate

❑ $1,000 Benefactor

❑ $500 Patron

❑ $250 Leader

❑ $100 Sponsor

❑ $50 Individual

❑ $40 CPITS Poet-Teacher

Your contribution is tax-deductible and includes the CPITS' annual statewide student and poet-teacher anthology. Please make checks payable to CPITS, 1333 Balboa Street, Suite 3, San Francisco, CA 94118.
For credit card payment please fill out the form below:

Name _____
(as it appears on your credit card)

Address _____

City/State/Zip _____

Date _____ Phone _____

Signature _____ Card expires _____

VISA/MC/Amex# _____

California Poets in the Schools can be contacted at:
Phone: 415-221-4201
Toll Free: 1-877-274-8764
Email: info@cpits.org — Visit our Website: www.cpits.org